Daring to Be Different

BY JUDITH COUCHMAN

Bible Studies
Daring to Be Different: A Study on Deborah
Becoming a Woman God Can Use: A Study on Esther
Entrusting Your Dreams to God: A Study on Hannah
Choosing the Joy of Obedience: A Study on Mary
Celebrating Friendship
His Gentle Voice (Bible study in the book)
Designing a Woman's Life Bible Study
Why Is Her Life Better Than Mine?
If I'm So Good, Why Don't I Act That Way?
Getting a Grip on Guilt

Books
The Shadow of His Hand
His Gentle Voice
A Garden's Promise
The Woman Behind the Mirror
Shaping a Woman's Soul
Designing a Woman's Life
Lord, Please Help Me to Change
Lord, Have You Forgotten Me?

Compilations
Encouragement for the Heart
Psalm 23
Amazing Grace
Voices of Faith
Promises for Spirit-Led Living
Cherished Thoughts about Friendship
Cherished Thoughts about Love
Cherished Thoughts about Prayer
Breakfast for the Soul
One Holy Passion

Life Messages of Great Christians Series
His Redeeming Love (Jonathan Edwards)
The Way of Faith (Martin Luther)
Growing in Grace (John Wesley)
Called to Commitment (Watchman Nee)
The Promise of Power (Jamie Buckingham)
Only Trust Him (Dwight L. Moody)
For Me to Live Is Christ (Charles Spurgeon)
Growing Deeper with God (Oswald Chambers)
Dare to Believe (Smith Wigglesworth)
Anywhere He Leads Me (Corrie ten Boom)
Loving God with All Your Heart (Andrew Murray)
A Very Present Help (Amy Carmichael)

WOMEN OF FAITH
BIBLE STUDY SERIES

Women of the Bible

Daring to Be Different

A Study on Deborah

Judith Couchman

Foreword by Barbara Johnson
Fiction by RuthAnn Ridley

ZONDERVAN
GRAND RAPIDS, MICHIGAN 49530 USA

ZONDERVAN™

Daring to Be Different
Formerly titled *Deborah*
Copyright © 1999 by Women of Faith, Inc.

Judith Couchman, General Editor

Requests for information should be addressed to:

Zondervan, *Grand Rapids, Michigan 49530*

ISBN 0-310-24781-0

All fiction works about Deborah are by RuthAnn Ridley, © 1988 by RuthAnn Ridley. Used by permission of the author.

Material quoted from *Nelson's New Illustrated Bible Dictionary* used by permission of Thomas Nelson, Inc.

All Scripture quotations, unless otherwise indicated, are taken from the *Holy Bible: New International Version*®. NIV®. Copyright © 1973, 1978, 1984 by International Bible Society. Used by permission of Zondervan. All rights reserved.

All rights reserved. No part of this publication may be reproduced, stored in a retrieval system, or transmitted in any form or by any means—electronic, mechanical, photocopy, recording, or any other—except for brief quotations in printed reviews, without the prior permission of the publisher.

Interior design by Sherri Hoffman

Printed in the United States of America

02 03 04 05 06 07 / ❖ CH/ 10 9 8 7 6 5 4 3 2

*For Anne Scott,
a spiritual warrior*

Contents

Acknowledgments   9

Foreword   11

About This Study   13

Introduction   17

SESSION ONE: One of a Kind   19
   Daring to be different for God.

SESSION TWO: Plain and Simple   28
   Choosing to speak the Lord's words.

SESSION THREE: The Need to Lead   37
   Stepping out when others won't.

SESSION FOUR: The Big Chance   45
   Recognizing when the time is right.

SESSION FIVE: A Humble Success   54
   Giving the praise to the Almighty.

SESSION SIX: Good Memories   63
   Encouraging people with your story.

Leader's Guide   71

About the Authors   76

Acknowledgments

Many thanks to Ann Spangler at Zondervan for giving me the opportunity to write about Deborah, and to Christine Anderson and Lori Walburg for their expert editing. A debt of gratitude goes to RuthAnn Ridley for graciously contributing her creative fiction pieces on Deborah. Also to Charette Barta, Opal Couchman, Win Couchman, Madalene Harris, Karen Hilt, Shirley Honeywell, and Nancy Lemons — all women who are available to God, especially through prayer.

Others who prayed and must be thanked are Joan Badzik, Betty Bradley, Jan Condon, Kathy Fisher, Tammy Holliday, Karen Howells, Linda Kraft, Mae Lammers, Beth Lueders, Marian McFadden, Cindy Miller, Victoria Munro, Kay O'Connor, Arlene Ord, Rita Rocker, Naomi Smith, Connie Swanson, Mary Jane Tynan, Lucibel VanAtta, and Kathe Wunnenberg. They are a prayer team to be reckoned with in the heavens.

Foreword

I love a woman who can exit the rigors of a battle singing! Deborah is just that kind of gal, and that makes me eager to take a closer look at her life. In this world riddled with relational conflicts, time crunches, and inescapable responsibilities, I often suffer from battle fatigue. I've even entertained going AWOL, but where does one go AWOL to? Although in the midst of life's pressures I have at times experienced sweet joy and indescribable peace, it isn't often that a song rises in my heart despite my circumstances.

Deborah was a woman who wore many hats, so she understood time crunches and inescapable responsibilities. She also helped mediate relational conflicts, which tells me she dealt with her share of feisty opposition. And I find I am much more likely to hear the words of a song sung by someone who has been there and done that, rather than by someone who is just vocalizing. Deborah's well-traveled sandals hiked from the valley of reality to the mountaintop of victory. Go, girl! She knows the way and is willing to lead. Now the big question is, Will we follow? Valleys can be the pits and mountaintops, as glorious as the views may eventually be, are initially a threat to scale. It's going to take courage to follow Deborah, but then any worthwhile path does take some moxie.

Before us lies an arduous adventure as we watch firsthand Deborah's challenges and triumphs. We will see the rough terrain of relationships and the refreshing responses of righteousness. And we will hear the glorious melody of music birthed in the midst of opposition and persecution.

I love a woman who exits the rigors of a battle singing, and I believe you, too, admire that kind of tenacity. We all long for examples, heroines, experienced guides, which is why I so love the ladies from Scripture. They were winsome women who exhibited wisdom even as warriors. So come, join me as we slip into Deborah's sandals and walk awhile on her rocky path. Along the way I believe we will be heartened in our own life-traverse, to awaken and sing unto the Lord a new song.

—*Patsy Clairmont*

About This Study

*E*veryone loves a captivating story. It can prompt laughter, tears, nods of the head, even thoughtful silence. Best of all, a good story teaches us how to live better. It doles out guidelines, points to pitfalls, and inspires us toward heart-changing action. It infuses the ordinary with meaning and the tragic with truth.

In this Women of Faith discussion guide you'll explore one of those poignant stories. Through the life of Deborah, a biblical woman with a challenging mission, you'll learn how God can work in the world, in the lives of his people, and in your circumstances. Each of the six sessions unfolds her story, compares it to yours, and initiates a group discussion that hopefully invokes spiritual growth and life-related applications.

To most effectively utilize this discussion guide with your group, consider organizing your time as follows.

BEFORE THE GROUP SESSION

Before attending a meeting, take time alone to evaluate your life and prepare for the next group discussion. During this time read and ponder the following sections of the discussion guide.

- *Opening Narrative.* Each week you'll be ushered into another chapter of Deborah's story. This fiction narrative introduces her unusual circumstances and helps you envision how Deborah felt, and perhaps what she did, as the events around her unfolded. It can get you thinking about the story before the group assembles, and whet your appetite for what happens next.
- *Setting the Stage.* Based on Deborah's story and the session's theme, think about your life. The questions and suggested activities can help you consider the following: How am I doing in this area? How do I feel about it? What do I want to do or change? How does this affect my spiritual life? Be honest with yourself and God, asking him to teach you through Deborah's story.

DURING YOUR TIME TOGETHER

The heart of this guide focuses on gathering together for discussion and encouragement. It allows time to study the Bible, apply its truths to your lives, and spend time praying. Of course, you can add whatever else fits the nature of your group, such as time for a "coffee klatch" or catching up on each other's lives. Whatever you decide, reserve about an hour for the next four sections.

- *Discussing Deborah's Story.* In this section read and discuss a biblical passage that captures the remarkable events of Deborah's life. Though the discussion centers on the facts of God's Word, at times you'll read between the lines and suggest people's feelings, motivations, and character qualities to gain insights to their actions. Still, you can answer these questions without compromising the biblical text.

    To best manage this discussion time, you can follow these steps:

    1. Ask one woman to read out loud the fiction narrative, if it seems appropriate. If not, skip this step.
    2. As a group read aloud the Bible passage stated at the beginning of the section. Take turns reading verses so each woman participates.
    3. Discuss the questions together, consulting specific verses from the text as needed.

- *Behind the Scenes.* This section provides background information related to the biblical text. It enlightens the story's culture and history, and helps you answer the discussion questions. You can refer to this section as you discuss Deborah's story.

- *Sharing Your Story.* How does Deborah's story apply to your life? As a group you can answer the questions in this section, relating the events of her life to your own and uncovering nuggets of practical application. These questions target group sharing rather than personal contemplation.

- *Prayer Matters.* To conclude your session use these ideas to guide the group in prayer, especially focusing on individual needs.

AFTER A MEETING

Since spiritual growth doesn't end with your small group gathering, try these suggestions to extend learning into the next week and encourage one-on-one relationships. However, these sections are optional, depending on your interest and schedule.

- *After Hours.* These activities help apply the lesson's principles to everyday life. You can complete them with a friend or by yourself.
- *Words to Remember.* After you return home, consider memorizing the selected Bible verse for encouragement and guidance.

In addition, the back of this book presents a Leader's Guide to help your group's facilitator pilot the discussion. To insure that everyone contributes to the conversation, it's best to keep the group at six to eight participants. If the membership increases, consider splitting into smaller groups during the discussion times and gathering together for the concluding prayer.

However you organize the meeting, keep the emphasis on discussion — sharing ideas, needs, and questions, rather than striving for a consensus of opinion. That's the pleasure of a good story. It stimulates thinking and reflects our inner selves, so along with Deborah we can become women of faith.

—*Judith Couchman, General Editor*

Introduction

Deborah was different from most women in ancient Israel. She was different from many women today.

Deborah was different for God, and in a faithless world, that sets anybody apart. It also makes life exciting.

When we commit ourselves to God and his will, anything can happen. We find ourselves saying and doing things we'd never imagined. We observe God working in miraculous ways. We participate in the redemption of his people. We feel joy. We marvel at the Lord.

That's what happened to Deborah. God equipped Deborah with leadership gifts and positioned her to use them. She's introduced in the Old Testament as a prophetess and a judge who rules Israel during a chaotic time. A Canaanite king has oppressed the Israelites for twenty years, and they finally cry out to the Lord. God tells Deborah it's time to fight the enemy and be delivered, and an intriguing story of partial obedience and missed opportunities, courage and deception, unfolds. Despite it all, God accomplishes his will: the Israelites defeat the enemy and live in peace for forty years. All because Deborah heard God's call and chose to follow it.

But what does her story have to do with us? Most of us won't be prophets, judges, or leaders of nations. In fact, we feel ordinary and unnoticed. What we forget is that following God makes us different — from unbelievers, but also from one another. God has created each of us uniquely and for a specific purpose. And in that purpose we can dare to accomplish what he asks of us.

In that purpose, too, we'll find ourselves leading in one way or another. Perhaps not as presidents or judges (though some of us will!), but certainly as mothers, managers, employees, performers, professionals, business owners, ministry directors, intercessors, Sunday school teachers, community volunteers, and more. Whatever our God-endowed roles in life, being "separated unto the Lord" distinguishes us as women of faith and influence.

Still, how do we begin? In the next weeks as your group follows Deborah's story, you'll discuss concepts that can set a woman apart from the crowd and build a foundation for pursuing God's directives, his way. In the six sessions you'll learn about:

- Understanding what it means to be different for God.
- Choosing to speak the Lord's words, even when it's difficult.
- Stepping out when others won't take a stand for him.
- Waiting for and recognizing God's timing for you.
- Turning praise away from yourself and onto others.
- Encouraging others spiritually with your story.

In a world where most people look out for themselves, these discussion times will help you look, instead, to God. Then you can begin living differently for him.

—Judith Couchman

SESSION ONE

One of a Kind

Daring to be different for God.

As the sun rose, a shaft of light fell across the reclining figure. Deborah turned over and tried to sleep, but it was useless. Finally she gave up, rolled up her mat, and lit the charcoal brazier in a corner of the room.

She thought about the news she'd heard the day before. There had been another kidnapping — a young girl and her brother. The Canaanite oppression was becoming unbearable. Anyone who ventured to the watering places feared the sudden thundering of iron chariots, bringing the archers who killed for sport.

When Deborah was a girl, many of her people had lived in unwalled hamlets. The children had spent summer afternoons playing at the wells. But Sisera and his chariots had changed all that.

Now the hamlets looked like ghost towns. Cooking pots lay broken and covered with dust. The wind blew children's toys across empty game squares. Families had left their homes to live in fortressed cities.

Deborah hated to think what might happen to the boy and girl who had been captured. Tears rolled down her cheeks. She gave in to crying for a few minutes, then drew her sleeve across her face. *This is no way for a judge to behave,* she thought. *You have work to do.*

As she pinned up graying hair under her head covering, she wondered why God hadn't made her like other women, content with grandchildren, embroidery, and gossip with friends. Instead, she had unusual ideas and insights. She had learned to act on intuition — the gleam of light that sometimes flashed across her mind. And now she was a judge of Israel. She was different — different for God. She liked that, though at times some people wanted to "put her in her place."

Deborah ate a few bites of the cake of ground dates she'd made the day before and broke off a piece to take with her. She was ready to begin the day's work.

The moment she walked outside, she caught the morning sky's splendor. The colors! Mauve, peach, almost yellow. She felt a sudden awe, a hush, and bowed her head to whisper words of praise. Calmed now and joyful, she began climbing the hill toward the palm tree. Clusters of golden dates hung from it like huge bells. Underneath this palm tree, she listened to her people's grievances and judged their cases according to Jehovah's laws.

When Deborah reached the top of the hill, she settled under the tree and waited. Soon she spotted a small group of people on the road below. Voices traveled on the wind, loud and sharp. Two men gestured angrily as they climbed the hill. A woman and child walked behind them holding hands.

"Please, Lord," prayed Deborah. "Give me wisdom."

Setting the Stage

WHAT DOES DIFFERENT MEAN?

In the next weeks your group will study Deborah, a woman who dared to be different. Different from the "normal role" for women in her culture; different in values from the pagan beliefs surrounding her; different in the way she handled her success. But the most important difference was that she committed her life to God. Deborah was different not for herself, but for him.

How does someone become different — and make a difference — for God? Author and theologian C. S. Lewis explained it way:

> The Christian way is different: harder, and easier. Christ says, "Give me All. I don't want so much of your time and so much of your money and so much of your work: I want You. I have not come to torment your natural self, but to kill it. No half-measures are any good. I don't want to cut off a branch here and a branch there, I want to have the whole tree down. Hand over the whole natural self, all the desires which you think innocent as well as the ones you think wicked — the whole outfit. I will give you a

new self instead. In fact, I will give you Myself; my own will shall become yours."

Before attending the first group session, think about what "being different for God" means to you. Jot down your thoughts about these questions:

- To you, what does it mean to be different for God in your daily life?

- How do you feel about C. S. Lewis's definition of the "Christian way" being different? What would be hard about it? What would be easy?

- If you dared to be different for God, how might your life change?

- How would you like to make a difference for him?

Close this time with an honest prayer to God about how you feel about being different for him.

Discussing Deborah's Story

THE FIRST AND ONLY

Deborah was the first and only female judge in ancient Israel. That's quite an accomplishment by itself. Judges led the people, interpreted national laws, and commanded military forces. But Deborah also was fair, trustworthy, and God-fearing. These were hard-to-find attributes during the chaotic times recorded in the Old Testament book of Judges. Still, Deborah held firm, and dared to be different for God.

Before you begin the discussion, read the Bible text, Judges 4:1–5.

1. In verses 1–2, read about Israel's plight after the judge Ehud died. What kind of new leader did Israel need?

2. During this time, what roles did Deborah serve in her personal and professional life? See verses 4–5.

3. Read the Behind the Scenes section, "The Role of Judges," on page 24. What characteristics did Deborah need to be an effective and honorable judge of Israel?

4. What challenges did Deborah face leading the Israelites during this era?

5. As a judge, Deborah fulfilled an unusual position for a woman in her culture. How might she have garnered such universal respect from her people? Consider at least three possibilities.

Sharing Your Story

TAKING THE DARE

Even though Deborah lived thousands of years ago, her difficulties and victories represent the path of women who pursue God and his will. No matter the era, no matter the calling, the Lord asks us to "come out from them and be separate" (2 Corinthians 6:17). When we do, it's a distinctive journey.

1. Reread the Setting the Stage section "What Does Different Mean?" on pages 20–21, through the quote by C. S. Lewis. As a group, complete this sentence, writing it on a whiteboard or easel pad so everyone can see it. "Being different for God means . . ."

Behind the Scenes

THE ROLE OF JUDGES

Judges were military heroes or deliverers who led the nation of Israel against their enemies during the period between the death of Joshua and the establishment of kingship. The stories of their exploits are found in the book of Judges.

During the period of the judges, from about 1380–1050 B.C., the government of Israel was a loose confederation of tribes gathered about their central shrine, the ark of the covenant. Without a human king to guide them, the people tended to rebel and fall into worship of false gods time and time again. "Everyone did what was right in his own eyes" (Judges 17:6; 21:25) is how the book of Judges describes these chaotic times. To punish the people, God himself would send foreign nations or tribes to oppress the Israelites.

These judges or charismatic leaders would rally the people to defeat the enemy. As God's agents for justice and deliverance, they would act decisively to free the nation from oppression. But the judges themselves were often weak, and their work was short-lived. The people would enter another state of rebellion and idolatry, only to see the cycle of oppression and deliverance repeated all over again.

The judges themselves were a diverse lot. Some of them received only a brief mention in the book of Judges.... The careers of the other judges are explored in greater detail in the book of Judges. Othniel, a nephew of Caleb (3:7–11), was a warrior-deliverer who led the Israelites against the king of Mesopotamia. Ehud (3:12–30) was distinguished by left-handedness and his deftness with a dagger. Jephthah (11:1–12:7) was a harlot's son whose devotion to God was matched only by his rashness. Gideon (6:11–8:35) needed many encouragements to act upon God's call. But he finally led 300 Israelites to defeat the entire army of the Midianites. The

> most interesting of the judges, perhaps, was Samson (13:1–16:31), whose frailties of the flesh led to his capture by the hated Philistines. The most courageous of the judges was Deborah, a woman who prevailed upon Barak to attack the mighty army of the Canaanites (4:1–5:31).
>
> The stories of the judges make interesting reading because of their rugged personalities and the nature of the times in which they lived. The openness with which they are portrayed in all their weaknesses is one mark of the integrity of the Bible.
>
> — Ronald F. Youngblood,
> *Nelson's New Illustrated Bible Dictionary*

2. How can you distinguish between "being different for God" and being rebellious? For example, if you decide to "go against the crowd," how do you know whether you're following God's desire or your own?

3. In our culture, what challenges face a woman who dares to be different for God? How can you overcome these challenges? Write both lists on a whiteboard or easel pad.

4. What could be the benefits of being different for God? Divide into pairs and discuss this question. Then share your answers with the whole group, listing them on the board or easel pad. As a group, choose the top three benefits of being different for God.

In the next weeks you'll discover that for Deborah, following Jehovah was challenging and surprising, exciting and satisfying. God wants the same for you. So get ready. Take the dare. Become different for God.

Prayer Matters

LORD, I AM THINE

Finish today's session with a group prayer of dedication to God, expressing your desire to follow him. Begin by reading aloud in unison this prayer from a Methodist covenant service. Then each woman can add a short statement about how she desires to be different for God. Your leader can close with a brief prayer.

> *Dear Lord,*
> *I am no longer my own, but thine.*
> *Put me to what thou wilt, rank me with whom thou wilt:*
> *Put me to doing: put me to suffering:*
> *Let me be employed for thee, or laid aside for thee:*
> *Exalted for thee, or brought low for thee:*
> *Let me be full, let me be empty:*
> *Let me have all things: let me have nothing:*
> *I freely and heartily yield all things to thy pleasure and disposal.*
> *And now, O glorious and blessed God, Father, Son, and Holy Spirit,*
> *Thou art mine and I am thine. So be it.*
> *Amen.*

After Hours

DISTINCTLY DIFFERENT

God has already made you distinctly different from anyone else. This week, consider how this uniqueness can accomplish God's will for you and the world you live in.

With a friend: Plan to do something fun and "distinctly different for God" together. Something that detours from your usual routine and expresses God's love to the world. Take cookies to teachers at your child's school, offer to shape up an elderly person's yard, or volunteer at a nursing home. Or be unusual and offer to buy a stranger's meal at a fast-food restaurant or pool together and pay for a financially struggling person's utility bill. Be thoughtful and creative!

On your own: During your private time with God, pull out a piece of paper and a pencil. Place your palm on the paper, spread out your fingers, and trace around the hand with the pencil. On each outlined finger, write a talent or attribute that characterizes you.

Pray and ask God how you could use each characteristic for him. Then at the tip of each finger, write a few words that describe how you might use the corresponding trait to be different for God. For example, you could write "compassionate" on a finger and "invite homeless people for dinner" at the tip of it.

Keep the drawing in your Bible or journal. Choose one characteristic to begin with, but also prayerfully plan how to use all five traits for God.

Words to Remember

YOUR LIFE, GOD'S WILL

> Teach me to do your will,
> for you are my God;
> may your good Spirit
> lead me on level ground.
>
> — Psalm 143:10

SESSION ONE — *One of a Kind*

SESSION TWO

Plain and Simple

Choosing to speak the Lord's words.

One autumn night Deborah fell into a sleep troubled by the pounding of rain like hoofbeats over her head. Vivid images filled her dreams. Sisera, thundering into Harosheth, bending to kiss his mother, startled by the sound of trumpets from a high mountain; an Israelite general with a small army, challenging the mighty troops Sisera had gathered; chariots, kings, the clash of swords at the Kishon River; and a shining, terrifying presence like an angel of wrath among them.

The shifting scenes seemed to play for a long time. Then there was blackness . . . and a voice: "Deborah!"

"Yes, Lord? I am here."

"I want you to summon Barak."

The voice continued — stern, commanding, and yet somehow gentle. Then it faded into the background, and suddenly Deborah was awake.

Her husband, Lappidoth, lay still, his breathing deep and regular.

Deborah got up, wound a shawl about her, and strode outside. The rain had stopped. The smell of the wet earth mingled with the sense of a Mighty Presence. She stood still, listening. As she waited, a tiny flame sprang up inside her. It was the beginning of something new. She hurried back into the house, picked up the lamp from its stand, and paced back and forth, praying and thinking.

When morning arrived, Deborah took the bread dough out of the kneading trough, shaped it, and placed it on top of the embers in the small oven. The fragrance of the baking bread filled the room, and Lappidoth appeared, ready to eat.

Deborah told him about the vision.

He wiped his mouth with the back of his hand, broke off another piece of bread, and reached for the water. When he finally spoke, he pronounced, "It's just a dream. Forget about it."

For a moment Deborah sat still, her anger growing hot. Then she shoved her chair back from the table and stomped outside.

"Lord, I'm tired of complacency! Where is the man of action who listens for the voice of God, the leader who is willing to take a risk in spite of what people say? Where is the servant who will forget about his own comfort and obey you unconditionally? Am I the only one who will speak your words?"

Then it came to her. *Barak!*

"Will Barak listen to your command, Lord? I'll send for him today."

Setting the Stage

WHAT CAN I SAY?

When God asks somebody to speak up for him, the chosen person isn't always ready and willing. Take, for example, Moses, who argued with God (Exodus 3:1–4:17), or Jonah, who ran away from him (Jonah 1:1–3). In fact, it's a frequent human response to tell the Lord, for one reason or another, that we'd be inept at representing him.

Exodus 4:10–12 records Moses' main objection to speaking up for God:

> Moses said to the LORD, "O Lord, I have never been eloquent, neither in the past nor since you have spoken to your servant. I am slow of speech and tongue."
>
> The LORD said to him, "Who gave man his mouth? Who makes him deaf or mute? Who gives him sight or makes him blind? Is it not I, the LORD? Now go; I will help you speak and will teach you what to say."

What if God asked you to speak for him? In the spaces below, record your objections and inadequacies, and imagine God's responses. If there is a current situation in which God is already asking you to speak out, focus on it. Complete the exercise before attending your group meeting.

God: *I want you to speak for me about . . .*

Your objection:

God's reply:

Your inadequacies:

SESSION TWO – *Plain and Simple*

God's reply:

Your response:

God's reply:

In this week's session you'll observe how Deborah spoke up with God's words to Barak and eventually changed her nation's history.

Discussing Deborah's Story

A CONFIDENT COMMAND

If Deborah's job could be summed up in a word, it'd be *spokesperson*. She was God's mouthpiece to Israel as she sat under the palm tree, dispensing wisdom. She also spoke for God when the people needed to defend themselves against wicked King Jabin.

Deborah was so confident in her role, she told Barak, the nation's military leader, "The LORD, the God of Israel, *commands* you" (emphasis added). This judge knew not only what to say, but how to say it.

Before you begin the discussion, read the Bible text, Judges 4:6–10.

1. Read the Behind the Scenes section, "Speaking for God," on page 32. What privileges would accompany being God's spokesperson? What would be the pitfalls?

2. Why would Deborah possess the confidence to summon Barak, a military leader (verse 6)?

DEBORAH — *Daring to Be Different for God*

3. In verse 8, why would Barak decline to go into battle without Deborah?

4. What was the significance of Deborah's reply to Barak in verse 9?

5. Hearing Deborah's reply, how would Barak feel? What might he have said?

6. Why would Barak still go into battle with Deborah?

Behind the Scenes

SPEAKING FOR GOD

Israel's ongoing pattern of disobedience, alien oppression, cries for help, and God's sovereign deliverance had been repeated over and over again by the time we gain a glimpse of Deborah — wife, poet, prophetess, Israel's appointed leader, and its first and only female judge.

We first see her sitting under a palm tree, settling disputes. The tree, which came to be named for her — the Palm of Deborah — was located in the hill country of Ephraim, about eight miles north of what would one day be known as Jerusalem. She held court there, overlooking a rock-covered vista of shrubs and bluffs.' . . .

Hour after hour, sitting under the unrelenting sun . . . Deborah listened before she spoke. Presenting their cases before their judge, Israel's men and women were confident they would receive fair treatment. They accepted her lucid decisions with respect, if not always with gratitude. The Hebrews trusted Deborah's words because they believed she represented God's active interest in Israel. To them, Lappidoth's wife was the Lord's sole spokesperson.

Deborah was the only judge of Israel who would be called a prophet — a foreteller and forthteller — someone to whom God gave specific knowledge of future events and divinely inspired words of instruction and correction, who then made this information known publicly. She was also the only woman in the Old Testament history who would rise to the pinnacle of political power by the people's common consent.

— Debra Evans, *Women of Courage*

Sharing Your Story

GOOD RIDDANCE TO RESERVATIONS

You can be God's spokeswoman. He wants each of us to speak for him, communicating his love, forgiveness, and redemption to others. But first we may need to work through our questions and reservations if we don't feel qualified or ready.

Can he really use us? Even in difficult situations?

The answer is yes, if we're willing ...

1. Women can have trouble speaking up and/or saying what they really think. Why would this be so? Name several reasons, listing them on a whiteboard or easel pad.

2. In addition, why are we reluctant to speak up for God? Add these reservations to the list. Remember that speaking up for God doesn't usually mean announcing, "Thus said the Lord ..." It can be speaking God's truth and values in a situation, offering comforting words in times of pain, being honest when it's tempting to lie, etc.

3. How can we overcome our uneasiness about speaking up for God? Write out suggestions for each "reluctance" you've listed.

SESSION TWO – *Plain and Simple*

4. How can we be sure we're speaking God's words and not our own opinions? For example, if we tell a friend she's chosen by God for a certain mission, how can we know we're sensing the Lord's will and not our own best wishes for her? Or, if we chastise someone, how can we tell if we're not just speaking from our own hurt or jealousy?

5. Share a time when someone spoke God's words to you. How did it affect you? Did the words change anything in your life? What was the outcome?

6. Share a time when you spoke God's words to someone else. What happened? What did you learn from that experience?

    To speak up for God, we don't have to start with lots of people or the big battles of life. We can begin one on one, in the quiet, everyday moments. In fact, the quantity of listeners we address at one time doesn't matter. It's the quality that counts. That means speaking the Lord's words, his way.
    Are you willing?

Prayer Matters

LORD, SPEAK TO ME

Use words from the hymn "Lord, Speak to Me, That I May Speak" by Frances R. Havergal to conduct your closing prayer time. Designate two women to each read aloud a stanza from the hymn. After reader #1 recites the first stanza, each group member can say a simple prayer that begins with, "Lord, speak to me about..." After reader #2 says the second stanza, group members can each pray, "Lord, use me to..."

To close your prayer time, an additional reader #3 can offer the final benediction.

Reader #1:
Lord, speak to me, that I may speak
In living echoes of Thy tone:
As Thou hast sought, so let me seek
Thy erring children lost and lone.

Each Woman:
Lord, speak to me about...

Reader #2:
O use me, Lord, use even me,
Just as Thou wilt, and when and where;
Until Thy blessed face I see,
Thy rest, Thy joy, Thy glory share.

Each Woman:
Lord, use me to...

Reader #3:
Lord, we offer these prayers to you.
Please hear and answer them.
Teach us to speak for you. Amen.

SESSION TWO – *Plain and Simple*

After Hours

MIND YOUR MOUTH

To speak up for God, we need to "mind our mouths" so they communicate clearly and don't inadvertently wound others. So this week, begin shoring up your communication skills.

With a friend: Read a chapter from a book about improving your communication skills: speaking, writing, witnessing, or relating to others. Discuss how the specific principles could help you communicate God's words to others.

On your own: This week look for ways to speak positive words to people. Rather than taking an opportunity to criticize or complain, say something uplifting or encouraging. Later, jot down what you said and how people responded. At the end of the week, review how your positive words affected others for the better.

Words to Remember

TALKING IT UP

> I do not hide your righteousness in my heart;
> I speak of your faithfulness and salvation.
> I do not conceal your love and your truth from the great assembly.
>
> — Psalm 40:10

SESSION THREE

The Need to Lead

Stepping out when others won't.

$\mathcal{M}$ost of the men who responded to Barak's summons were from Naphtali, Zebulun, and Issachar. Crudely armed with clubs and axes, many worked as woodcutters in Harosheth.

Barak informed Deborah when the number of men in the army reached 10,000. Then they began the march to Mount Tabor. Although the mountain was only 1,800 feet above sea level, it provided an extensive view and a vantage point from which they could rush down upon the Canaanites.

When the Israelites reached the top, Barak set up headquarters behind the ruins of an ancient fortress. To the south they could see Mount Gilboa, and to the north the snowcapped Mount Hermon. Deborah walked with Barak through the camp, encouraging the men.

The Israelite soldiers had been on Mount Tabor less than a day when they heard Sisera's chariots thundering across the plain. Deborah and Barak watched as the enemy mobilized below them on the banks of the Kishon River. Then the infantry poured in from every direction.

When night fell, Barak urged Deborah to get some rest. Exhausted, she slept without dreams, then suddenly woke up. It was still dark. She stumbled outside to find Barak still at his post, pacing. As far as the eye could see, glittering campfires dotted the black night.

"There's no way we can gain the victory over that many men," said Barak. His tone sounded flat.

Deborah hesitated before she spoke. *I'm not the one who has to risk my life on the battlefield,* she thought. *But I know God is at work.*

"You're right," she said. "It looks impossible, but God is with us. He will make a way."

They talked a while longer, and Barak finally felt enough peace to sleep. Deborah lay near her fire, wrapped in a cloak, and thought about how hard it was to wait. But learning to wait on God was essential; one's own wisdom never sufficed ...

Before dawn Deborah tiptoed past sleeping soldiers and gazed at the sky, thinking about the battle. Suddenly a dark cloud enveloped the hillside and stormed toward the river. Lightning flashed and balls of fire shot through the darkness. Water rained down from the sky.

Deborah raced to Barak's tent. "It's time, Barak," she yelled. "This is the day the Lord has given Sisera into your hands!"

Setting the Stage

UNNATURAL BORN LEADERS

Some of us are natural leaders. Others are not. But at times we all may need to set an example, organize an event, or "rally the troops." With our families, on the job, in the church or community, we can — sometimes unexpectedly or unwillingly — fulfill the leadership role. In our own way, we step out and influence others.

For each of the questions that follow, mark where your response to leadership falls on the accompanying gauge. For example, in question #1, if you are somewhere between "ready" and "reluctant," make an "x" mark between those two choices.

1. What is your response to being asked to lead?

Ready	Reluctant	Refusing

2. How do you feel about leading others?

Confident	Concerned	Confused

3. How many leadership roles do you fulfill now?

Many	Moderate	Miniscule

Whether or not you're a born leader, God wants to use you to spiritually affect others. In fact, he specializes in turning weak and fearful people into remarkable influencers. When you gather with the group this week, remember that you don't have to be a strong-willed "Deborah" to step out and make a difference for God. You can be you. You are enough for what he asks you to do.

Whatever your propensity toward leadership, how might God be asking you to step out and influence others? Write a few sentences about it below.

Discussing Deborah's Story

TAKING ON THE TROOPS

The Bible doesn't indicate why Barak wouldn't go into battle without Deborah. Nor does it provide her response. Was she frustrated with Barak? Understanding of his need to take the nation's leader with him? Nobody knows. But we do know this: God commanded the Israelites to battle their enemies. Since Deborah wasn't about to disobey the Lord, she did what was necessary. She agreed to "take on the troops" with Barak, and that was no easy task.

Before you begin the discussion, read the Bible text, Judges 4:11–17.

1. Deborah traveled with her nation's troops to the battlefield, from her home between Rahmah and Bethel to Mount Tabor. What does this indicate about her as a leader?

2. Compare Sisera's troops in verse 13 with Barak's in verse 14. If you were an Israelite soldier, what concerns would you have about the battle?

3. In verse 14 Deborah tells Barak to go into battle. If Barak was an accomplished military leader, why would he still wait for her command?

4. Why might Deborah exhort Barak with the words of verse 14?

5. The Behind the Scenes section, "Women in the Old Testament," on page 41 describes the usual role of women during Deborah's time. Why would the Israelite army accept leadership from a woman?

6. Why would the Lord have his people fight and kill the enemy "by the sword" instead of just wiping out Sisera's army by himself?

7. Verse 16 claims that "not a man was left" of Sisera's troops. Why was it important that every soldier died? See Deuteronomy 7:16 for insight.

Behind the Scenes

WOMEN IN THE OLD TESTAMENT

The position of women in Israel was in marked contrast with her status in surrounding nations. Israelite law was designed to protect women's weaknesses, safeguard her rights, and preserve her freedom (Deuteronomy 21:10–14; 22:13; 22:28). Under divine law her liberties were greater, her tasks more varied and important, and her social standing more respectful and commanding than that of her heathen sister. The Bible has preserved the memory of women whose wisdom, skill, and dignity it willingly acknowledged. Numerous names of devout and eminent Hebrew women adorn the pages of the Old Testament.

To some extent, a woman was her husband's property (Genesis 12:18; Exodus 20:17; 21:3) and owed him absolute fidelity. While the husband had no formal rights over the person of his wife, nevertheless, he was recognized as lord and master. By her chastity, diligence, and love, woman created an honorable position for herself within family and community circles.

Any prominence woman attained was obtained by force of character. There were those, like Deborah, who achieved greatness. Others, such as Esther, had greatness thrust upon them. Womanly virtues were foreign to pagan cultures under which women became subject to inferior and degrading conditions. Decline of women in Israel was always due to the invasion of heathen influences. Morality lapsed as idolatrous customs were countenanced.

— Herbert Lockyer, *All the Women of the Bible*

Sharing Your Story

THE FEAR OF FALLING

Are you ready to step out when others won't? Most of us don't feel like we are.

Thankfully, God prepares and empowers us to accomplish tasks beyond our expectations. Sometimes he quiets our fears about stepping out. Other times, we're to just do it, despite our emotions. However we feel, the Lord says he won't allow the righteous to plummet (Psalm 55:22). He understands and compensates for our fear of falling.

1. How do you feel about leading others? Share your responses to the Setting the Stage section, "Unnatural Born Leaders," on page 38.

2. In what ways might someone who doesn't consider herself a leader still need to lead?

3. When we risk influencing people, it can feel like stepping out onto thin air. So it's natural that we may feel afraid of falling. In what ways might we "fall" when influencing others?

4. How can we overcome our "fear of falling"?

5. How might being a follower of Christ require that you "step out" when others won't?

Whatever God asks us to step out and do, we can remember Deborah's words to Barak: "Has not the LORD gone ahead of you?" (Judges 4:14). God has promised that he'll lead us along unfamiliar paths and not forsake us (Isaiah 42:16). So when we face the need to lead others, we can follow after him!

Prayer Matters

LORD, LEAD ME

To step out for God, we need his guidance. In your group prayer time, each woman can ask the Lord for his leading in a situation specific to her. After each woman expresses her request aloud, the group can answer, "Yes, Lord. Lead [name of woman] in your way." The group could also lay hands on each woman as she prays and add individual prayers about her circumstances after she's finished.

Close the session by reading or singing these words in unison from the hymn "He Leadeth Me" by Joseph Gilmore.

> *He leadeth me! O blessed thought!*
> *O words with heav'nly comfort fraught!*
> *Whate'er I do, wheree'er I be,*
> *Still 'tis God's hand that leadeth me.*
> *He leadeth me, He leadeth me;*
> *By his own hand He leadeth me;*
> *His faithful foll'wer I would be,*
> *For by His hand He leadeth me.*

SESSION THREE — *The Need to Lead*

After Hours

FOLLOW THE LEADER

If you're uneasy about stepping out, it helps to prepare your path. This week plan how you can be an effective influencer.

With a friend: Choose a project or situation in which you need to step out and make a difference for God. Brainstorm and break each project into individual steps. (For example, if you want to work in a homeless shelter, break the "project" into (1) researching the various shelters; (2) making phone calls to the ones you're interested in; (3) setting up an interview; etc.) Create a visual aid for each step, such as footprints, and write a step on each footprint. Cut out the footprints and select one each week and tackle your project a step at a time. Your friend can do the same for her project. Check with each other periodically for a progress report. Celebrate when you complete your projects.

On your own: Whom do you admire as an influencer? Ask that person if you can "shadow" her or him for a day, observing the person in action. Schedule lunch together so you can ask prepared questions about leadership and risk taking.

Words to Remember

OUR FAITHFUL GUIDE

I will lead the blind by ways they have not known,
    along unfamiliar paths I will guide them;
I will turn the darkness into light before them
    and make the rough places smooth.
These are the things I will do;
    I will not forsake them.

— Isaiah 42:16

SESSION FOUR

The Big Chance

Recognizing when the time is right.

Jael lived in a tent near the mighty oak that stood three miles northeast of Mount Tabor. She'd watched Barak's army march toward the mountain and heard the thundering of Sisera's chariots.

The morning of the battle Jael dressed quickly, grabbed a handful of nuts, and ran down the rocky road near her tent. Her neighbors had already gathered to watch the battle. Women wept and tore their garments while old men stared in silence. Jael stood apart from the others, one hand lifted to catch the spattering rain.

Jael and her husband, Heber, were Kenites who had settled in the plain between Mount Tabor and Kedesh some years before. Heber had made a peace treaty with the Canaanite king, and his job as a metalworker enabled him and his wife to live well. Travelers told vivid tales of Jael's hospitality, her thick carpets, her beautiful pottery, and her fiery spirit.

When soggy Canaanite soldiers began fleeing toward Harosheth, the watchers scurried to their homes. But Jael lingered long enough to observe one soldier breaking away from the army.

She squinted. It was Sisera!

He musn't get away, she thought. Jael had always possessed a fondness for the Israelites and a respect for their God. Certainly they behaved better than the Canaanites. Sisera could be ruthless.

Would he come her way?

Somehow Jael knew the time was right for an encounter with Sisera. He would be beleaguered and needy. Now was the time to act courageously.

Setting the Stage

WHAT TIME IS IT?

An old but true cliché says that "timing is everything." When we pursue a task or mission, its success can depend on whether we're accomplishing it at the right time.

This is especially true of God's timing. We can rush ahead of his timing for us or lag behind it, missing the objective and blessing he intends. So learning to walk with God includes waiting for and recognizing his directives.

Is there something that God has asked you to do? If so, what could be his timing for you right now? Think about how he's prompted and led you, and determine what he wants you to be doing. Then draw hands on the clock below to show what "time" it is in the process to do this action. If it's 3:00, it's time to think and pray about it; if it's 6:00, it's time to learn about it; if it's 9:00, it's time to actively prepare for it; and if it's 12:00, it's time to act on it.

This is God's timing for me about _____.

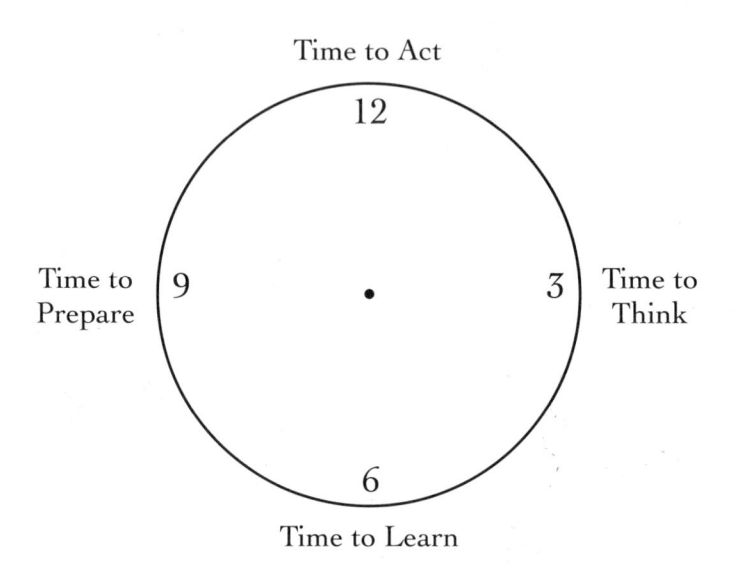

Time to Act

12

Time to Prepare — 9 · 3 — Time to Think

6

Time to Learn

DEBORAH — *Daring to Be Different for God*

Before attending this week's session, ponder these questions:

- As best you can tell, are you "on time" with God regarding this directive? What seem to be the indicators that you're on time?

- If you're lagging behind or rushing ahead of God's leading, what is the reason?

- How can you keep aligned with God's timing?

Discussing Deborah's Story

A STRIKE FOR ISRAEL

When Deborah told the reluctant Barak that "the Lord will hand Sisera over to a woman" (Judges 4:9), he probably thought the judge meant herself. But God had another female in mind — a woman who wasn't an Israelite. Jael, a member of the Kenite nation, recognized when the time was right to strike a blow for God's people. And unlike Barak, she didn't hesitate to act.

Before you begin the discussion, read the Bible text, Judges 4:17–24.

1. Based on this session's text, what type of woman was Jael? Name at least five characteristics.

2. The Behind the Scenes section, "When Might Was Right," on page 49 explains why Barak lost his chance to kill Sisera. Why would Jael gain this distinction? Do you agree with the Behind the Scenes author's opinion about Jael's method of murder? Why or why not?

3. Jael recognized when the time was right to destroy the enemy. If she'd missed the opportunity to strike, what might have happened?

4. When Barak saw the dead Sisera, what do you suppose he thought? Name a few possibilities.

5. Why would the author of Judges (possibly Samuel) state that "God subdued Jabin, the Canaanite king, before the Israelites" (verse 23), rather than "the Israelites subdued Jabin ... with God's help"?

Behind the Scenes

WHEN MIGHT WAS RIGHT

[Jael] was the wife of Heber the Kenite. The Kenites were not true Israelites, but were the descendents of Moses' wife.... From the first, perhaps because they remembered Moses' great deeds, the Kenites had sided with Israel.

Jael, too, was Israel's ally. She rejoiced when she heard of Barak's victory and would have wept had she heard that Sisera had defeated Israel with his chariots. Jael received the honor that Barak would like to have had. By her hand, as though by a judgment of God, Sisera, Israel's cruel oppressor, was killed. Barak would have had that honor just as David had that of slaying Goliath if he had not dallied and hesitated on the day Deborah, as a prophetess, told him the word of the Lord: "The journey that thou takest shall not be for thine honour, for the Lord shall sell Sisera into the hand of a woman" (Judges 4:9 KJV).

Therefore we may not disapprove of Jael's act in killing Sisera. We remember that an Israelite once took a harlot of the Midianites into his tent. On that occasion Phinehas pinned them together by a thrust of his javelin. For that he was praised because his zeal for Jehovah induced him to do it [Numbers 25:1–13]. Jael's act is no more censurable than his, for she was accomplishing the Lord's judgment upon Sisera. Hence it is written in Deborah's song: "Blessed above women shall Jael the wife of Heber the Kenite be, blessed shall she be above women in the tent."

—Abraham Kuyper, *Women of the Old Testament*

SESSION FOUR — *The Big Chance*

Sharing Your Story

MATTERS OF MOVEMENT

God's timing can't be reduced to a formula. At times he seems insufferably slow to act. At times he moves quickly. Sometimes he tells us when he's going to do something. Sometimes he surprises us. Still, the Lord wants us to keep our hearts "ready and willing" to participate with him when he prompts — or even commands — us to move ahead.

1. For you, what are the challenges of waiting for God's timing?

2. In contrast, what are the benefits of following God's timetable?

3. How can you tell when God is saying "the time is right" to do something?

4. What insights and encouragement can Psalm 31:15 and Isaiah 55:8–9 give you about waiting for God's timing?

5. What could cause us to miss God's timing?

6. If you think you've missed God's timing about something to say or do, what can you do about it now?

God's timing is accurate, though it often doesn't fit our expectations. "But do not forget this one thing, dear friends: With the Lord a day is like a thousand years, and a thousand years are like a day. The Lord is not slow in keeping his promise, as some understand slowness" (2 Peter 3:8–9). God acts at the right time. Don't miss acting with him.

Prayer Matters

LORD, SHOW ME

After the discussion, pray together about God's timing for specific situations in each woman's life. Then read aloud the following passage: Ecclesiastes 3:1–8, 11, 14. Group members can alternate reading the verses until they complete the passage. Ask one woman to close with a final prayer.

> [1] There is a time for everything, and a season for every activity under heaven:
>
> [2] a time to be born and a time to die, a time to plant and a time to uproot,
>
> [3] a time to kill and a time to heal, a time to tear down and a time to build,

⁴a time to weep and a time to laugh, a time to mourn and a time to dance,

⁵a time to scatter stones and a time to gather them, a time to embrace and a time to refrain,

⁶a time to search and a time to give up, a time to keep and a time to throw away,

⁷a time to tear and a time to mend, a time to be silent and a time to speak,

⁸a time to love and a time to hate, a time for war and a time for peace....

¹¹He has made everything beautiful in its time. He has also set eternity in the hearts of men; yet they cannot fathom what God has done from beginning to end....

¹⁴I know that everything God does will endure forever; nothing can be added to it and nothing taken from it. God does it so that men will revere him.

After Hours

THE TIMES OF YOUR LIFE

Looking at the past can help us trust God for his timing in the future. This week, remember the times of your life and how he's worked through them.

With a friend: Draw a spiritual timeline of your life. Designate the major time periods and how God worked in your life during each one. Invite a trusted friend to meet with you for coffee or lunch and share your timeline with her. If she's willing, ask her to answer these questions: In what ways do you see God has worked in my life? Do you see any themes or patterns? If so, what are they? From what you know about me and my story, what might the time be right for now?

Your friend might also draw a timeline so you can answer the same questions for her. Pray together about God's direction for each other.

On your own: Spend time with God in prayer, asking him to show you his will for your future. Then dream a little and continue the timeline exercise you began with a friend. Chart what you hope the times of your life will be from now until you reach heaven. Tuck the timeline in your Bible and periodically pray about and update it.

Words to Remember

TRUST AT ALL TIMES

Trust in him at all times, O people;
> pour out your hearts to him,
> for God is our refuge.

— Psalm 62:8

SESSION FIVE

A Humble Success

Giving the praise to the Almighty.

Jael pointed to the covered body lying crumpled on the floor. "This is the enemy," she said to Barak and Deborah. Without warning, she stooped down and threw back the blanket.

Deborah gasped.

Jael didn't seem to notice. She began describing every bloody detail of her conquest. When she finished, they all stood silently. Finally Deborah said, "You have been willing and bold. I'm glad you are not our enemy."

Jael chuckled and relaxed. Her voice softened. "I hope your Jehovah is pleased..."

Deborah left the tent just before sunset. She wanted to be alone. She had to think. She thought about her ancestor Miriam who'd led the women in praise after God parted the Red Sea. They'd danced and played tambourines. The Lord deserved that kind of celebration for saving the nation again. But it had to be done soon, while the victory was fresh.

When Barak returned to camp, Deborah told him the next day would be a time of praise and worship. They discussed the battle again, and Barak explained how the Lord had led him, making a way through the enemy's clashing swords.

Barak's revelation inspired Deborah. She wrote late into the night, creating the song she and the soldiers would sing. The words flowed. She felt as though they were being given to her, and yet they rose from deep within her soul.

She wrote better than she knew how.

When the princes in Israel take the lead,
when the people willingly offer themselves —
praise the LORD!
Hear this, you kings! Listen, you rulers!
I will sing to the LORD, I will sing;
I will make music to the LORD, the God of Israel.

Setting the Stage

PRAISEWORTHY MOMENTS

Remember this childhood ditty? *Sticks and stones may break my bones but words will never hurt me.* Remember when you learned that it wasn't true?

Words do affect us. We remember when people criticize or wound us. But we can also remember and feel nurtured by their praise. Before this week's session, think about the praiseworthy moments of your life.

- What is the greatest compliment someone ever gave you?

- Why did this expression of praise mean so much to you?

- From whom do you want praise the most? Why?

- How can you let this person know you need his or her praise?

- How can you become a better praise-giver yourself?

Our longing for appreciation patterns after God's desire for praise from us, especially when he's acted on our behalf. Deborah understood this and gave glory to God for his mighty works. In this session you'll discuss how praise can change and deepen your relationship with the Lord.

SESSION FIVE – *A Humble Success*

Discussing Deborah's Story

A SONG TO REMEMBER

Deborah contributed significant talents to her nation's well-being, but her greatest bequest centered on pointing others to the Lord. After the Israelite's victory in battle, she and Barak could have garnered all of the credit — and most likely, nobody would have begrudged them. But with a song, Deborah humbly recalled God's intervention and praised him for it, setting an example for her people, and for us.

Before you begin the discussion, read the Bible text, Judges 5:1–12.

1. Deborah began her song of praise with, "When the princes in Israel take the lead, when the people willingly offer themselves" (verse 2). Why would she begin with this observation and consider it a time to praise the Lord?

2. Verses 4–5 flash back to the Israelites' trek through the wilderness. According to these verses, God provided his people with water. Why would Deborah mention this?

3. Review verses 6–8. Before the battle led by Deborah and Barak, what had life been like for Israel? Who had created the problem?

DEBORAH — *Daring to Be Different for God*

Behind the Scenes

THE PURPOSE OF PRAISE

A number of different Hebrew words are used in the Old Testament to express the concept of praise. The common elements in these words focus our attention on the true nature of praise:

(1) Praise is addressed to God or his "name." God himself, his attributes, or his acts are the content of our thoughts, words, and songs.

(2) Praise is linked with the believing community's joy in the person of God. Most praise in the Old Testament is corporate, although an individual certainly could praise God in private. Most praise comes from those who are filled with a sense of joy in who God is and in how deeply he is committed to his people.

(3) Praise exalts the Lord. It is in praise that the believer implicitly acknowledges creaturely dependence on God and explicitly acknowledges God's greatness and goodness.

Several central Hebrew terms give us these insights.

- *Halal* means "to acclaim," "to boast of," "to glory in." It expresses our deep satisfaction in exalting the wonderful acts and qualities of the one being expressed.
- *Yadah* is translated "to praise," "to give thanks," and "to confess." It focuses on our acknowledgment of God's works and character, often in contrast with human failures.
- *Zamar* means "to sing praise," "to make music." It focuses on who God is and what he has done. It is found only in Bible poetry, usually in the Psalms.
- *Sabah* means "to praise or commend." Again, this is praise directed to the Lord, this time rich with notes of adoration.

— Adapted from Larry O. Richards,
Expository Dictionary of Bible Words

SESSION FIVE – *A Humble Success*

4. Deborah also described herself and her relationship to Israel (verses 7 and 9). Suggest at least two ways a contemporary reader could interpret her tone and meaning. Which interpretation do you think is correct?

5. The Behind the Scenes section on page 57 explains "The Purpose of Praise." How are the four Hebrew terms for praise (*halal, yadah, zamar, sabah*) evident in Deborah's song? Write out the phrases that represent these types of praise on the chalkboard or easel pad.

6. Throughout their history, God not only desired the praise of his people, he commanded it. (See Deuteronomy 8:10.) Why would this be so?

Sharing Your Story

GOD'S GLORY, OUR GAIN

Like Deborah, when we praise God we showcase the credit and glory he deserves. But we also receive the benefits of praise. In this discussion time, consider how praise affects the person who gives God the applause.

1. Praise is a spontaneous response when God has blessed us with his power and goodness. But when else would it be important to praise the Lord? Discuss several scenarios, and why praising God would be beneficial. (For example, praising the Lord can lift our spirits when we're downhearted.)

2. In the following passage from *Mighty Prevailing Prayer* by Wesley L. Duewel, circle the blessings this author says we receive when we praise the Lord.

   The more you praise God, the more you become God-conscious and absorbed in His greatness, wisdom, faithfulness, and love. Praise reminds you of all that God is able to do and of great things He has already done. Faith comes through God's Word and through praise. Faith grows as you praise the Lord.

   Praise gives you the spirit of triumph and overcoming. Praise fires you with holy zeal. It lifts you above the battles to the perspective of God's throne. Praise cuts the enemy forces down to size. "If God is for us, who can be against us?" (Romans 8:31). What can man do when God is with you? (Psalm 118:6; Hebrews 13:6). God's angel hosts with us are more than all who oppose us (2 Kings 6:16).

3. Which of these benefits of praise are you most interested in receiving? Why?

4. Even if we received no "benefits" from giving God the glory, why would we still praise him?

5. Praising God is a learned behavior. How can you teach yourself to praise the Lord? How can you integrate praise into your everyday life?

The psalmist wrote, "Sing to the LORD, you saints of his; praise his holy name" (Psalm 30:4). Along with him we can learn to praise God and be blessed by it. You can begin today.

Prayer Matters

LORD, YOU ARE . . .

Celebrate the Lord together! Before you leave for home, spend time praising God for his amazing attributes. Complete this responsive reading aloud, based on a prayer of Francis of Assisi (1181–1226).

Leader: You are holy, Lord, the only God,
and your deeds are wonderful.
You are strong.

Group: You are great.
You are the Most High,
You, Holy Father, are
King of heaven and earth.

Leader: You are Three and One,

Group: Lord God, all good.
You are Good, all Good, supreme Good,
Lord God, living and true.

Leader: You are love,

Group: You are wisdom.
You are humility,
You are endurance.
You are rest,
You are peace.
You are joy and gladness.
You are justice and moderation.
You are all our riches,
And you suffice for us.

Leader: You are beauty.

Group: You are gentleness.
You are our protector,
You are our guardian and defender.
You are courage.
You are our heaven and our hope.

Leader: You are our faith,

Group: Our great consolation.
You are our eternal life,
Great and wonderful Lord,
God almighty,
Merciful Savior.
Amen.

After Hours

NOTES OF PRAISE

Glorifying God can be fun and fulfilling. This week begin learning to praise the Lord with these easy-to-do activities.

With a friend: Together, invite selected friends, your small group, or church members to a praise party. Pattern it after a Christmas caroling party, singing praise songs and hymns in someone's home, at a nursing home, or even throughout a neighborhood. Conclude the evening by joining hands and thanking God for his praiseworthiness.

Or, instead of singing, read praise psalms and hymns aloud. They can be read both by individuals and in unison as a group. Then spend time telling stories of God's goodness in your lives, and, together, praise him for each person's testimony.

On your own: Each day this week write a praise note to God. Write a sentence or two on an index card or small piece of paper that extols one of his attributes. (For example, his love, goodness, power, sovereignty, etc. A praise note could say, "Lord, I praise you for your mighty acts of power in the universe.") Read the note aloud to him, then post it somewhere you'll see it throughout the day.

Each day review all of the praise notes you've written up until then. By week's end, you'll feel blessed by the Lord's magnificence — and that all of his resources are available to you, his child.

Words to Remember

A GOOD THING

It is good to praise the LORD and make music to your name, O Most High.

— Psalm 92:1

SESSION SIX

Good Memories

Encouraging people with your story.

It's time to leave, thought Deborah as she surveyed the campsite. Barak didn't need her anymore. He'd grown in confidence and was eager to finish subduing the Canaanites. So at Deborah's suggestion, he appointed some soldiers to escort her home.

The winds blew gently and the weather remained clear. Deborah noted the trees along the way: a tall valonia oak standing alone, clumps of bushy terebinth with their penetrating scent, and seas of brushwood stretching to the horizon. On this victory journey, she felt special joy and gratefulness for each scenic detail of her land.

When she arrived home, tired but thankful, Lappidoth had already heard most of the news, and after a short talk he insisted that she rest. Drifting in and out of sleep, she heard him talking to the soldiers. Excitement tinged his voice. Deborah thought she heard him ask if there was any way he could help.

The next morning, despite the long trip, Deborah felt ready once more to set up her court.

Messengers brought good news from Barak. His plan to conquer the cities rimming the Esdraelon plain was successful. Because of Sisera's death, few Canaanites resisted him. Still, Deborah wondered about the families of the slain soldiers. She was glad she didn't have to bear the emotions of war all of the time. She enjoyed using her gifts among the people, even if it meant hearing their complaints.

For the rest of her life, Deborah stayed home and judged God's people with integrity. She was content with her power to influence them for good. And whenever she could, to whomever would listen, she retold the story of God's greatness in battle.

Read "Behind the Scenes" P66

Setting the Stage

THE ELEMENTS OF STORY

Everyone has a story to tell, especially those who walk with God. Through the years we experience his love, provision, and deliverance in new ways. It's natural to share such stories, and they can encourage Christians in their faith, even turn nonbelievers into believers.

If you had one story to tell about God's goodness to you, what would it be? Jot down the main elements of the story below. These would include:

- The events that led up to the situation:

- The problems that developed:

- The crisis point of the story:

- How the crisis was resolved:

- What you learned about God through this episode:

If you had three minutes to tell this story, what would you say? Rehearse in your mind how you would tell it. In this week's session, you'll be asked to share your story with group members. They will be blessed!

Discussing Deborah's Story

A BATTLE IN REVIEW

The second half of Deborah's song continues to praise God, but it also recounts the Israelites' plight, the battle, and the aftermath. Deborah recorded these details not only to relive and celebrate the victory, but also to encourage those not present on the scene. Even future generations could read her words and rejoice in the Lord.

Before you begin the discussion, read the Bible text, Judges 5:13–31.

1. One Bible commentator explained that during this era, it "was a time of tribal independence, for not all the tribes [of Israel] participated in the war against Sisera." How could this independence have contributed to Israel's difficulties before, during, and after the battle?

   Barak not sure who will come

2. In verses 13–18, Deborah named which tribes participated in the battle and which did not. Why would she do this?

   Should we do this?

3. What additional insight to the victory does Deborah's song provide? See verses 19–27.

SESSION SIX — *Good Memories*

Behind the Scenes

PASSING THE ORAL TRADITION

In the days before the invention of printing and books, information had to be memorized and passed from person to person and from generation to generation by word of mouth. Information about everything: how to do things like fighting a war or making a boat; the history of one's family and people; the origin of the world and of all that happens in it; how to behave and what to do in times of birth, marriage, illness, and death.

Most of this is so important for the survival and well-being of the people in question that the information was told in forms that could easily be remembered — such as myths, sagas, folk tales, legends, riddles, songs, and proverbs. This is why oral traditions change very little over time, as we can still see today in areas like parts of Africa and India.

Even in countries where books are plentiful, children at play recite rhymes that have varied little from generation to generation. Before the arrival of paper and books, memory and learning played a vital part, which is why oral tradition is remarkably stable. This is important when considering such things as the composition of the Pentateuch and the transmission of the words of Jesus before the Gospels were written down. In Judaism the written Torah of the Pentateuch is augmented by the oral Torah, culminating in collections known as the Mishnah and the Talmud.

— John Bowker, *The Complete Bible Handbook*

4. Why would the song include stanzas about Sisera's mother (verses 28–30)?

5. Ancient Israel depended on storytelling or sharing the "oral tradition." Read about this heritage-preserving process in the Behind the Scenes section, "Passing the Oral Tradition," on page 66. How does Deborah's song fit into this tradition?

6. What lessons could Deborah's song pass along to future generations?

Sharing Your Story

CAN YOU BELIEVE IT?

When we tell stories of God's goodness toward us, we grow in faith and praise. For this final session, recount personal "God stories" to one another and be encouraged.

1. Why do we enjoy telling stories to one another?

2. Why would storytelling be important to God?

3. How could you pattern after Deborah's song when telling a story about God's goodness to you? (For example, you could also briefly recall how God was good to your ancestors.) Suggest a few examples.

4. Divide into groups of three and tell one another the three-minute stories you developed in the Setting the Stage section. When one "storyteller" finishes, tell her what you find encouraging about her story.

We love a good story. So does God. You're part of the story of his generous and patient relationship with humanity. He desires that your episode of the eternal story be told again and again. Like the "old, old story" of redemption, your story will never lose its power to touch lives.

Prayer Matters

LORD, I RECALL

An Old Testament psalmist wrote, "I remember the days of long ago; I meditate on all your works and consider what your hands have done" (Psalm 143:5). To close the session, form a circle and join hands. Each woman can say a prayer that begins with "Lord, I recall when . . ." and then name a good thing the Lord did for her. When she finishes, the entire group can say aloud, "We thank you, Lord, and praise you for your goodness." After everyone has prayed, turn to a woman beside you and hug her.

After Hours

THIS DO IN REMEMBRANCE

This week, continue to remember the good things God has done for you.

With a friend: Hold a "memorial meeting" with a small group of friends, over lunch or coffee together, telling stories of God's goodness in your lives. You may want to review Deborah's story and read parts of her song before telling your stories.

On your own: Start a Book of Remembrance by yourself or with your family. Obtain a blank journal and record in it stories of answers to prayer, God's provision, his intervention, and other incidents that display his goodness to you. If you're doing this with family members, leave the book in a place where anyone can add to it at any time. Be sure to date the entries. Once a month before dinner or family devotions, review the book together, thanking God for his goodness to you.

Words to Remember

THE NEXT GENERATION

Let this be written for a future generation,
 that a people not yet created may praise the LORD.
—Psalm 102:18

Leader's Guide

These guidelines and suggested answers can help enhance your group's effectiveness. However, remember that many questions require opinions rather than "right" or "wrong" answers. Input is provided only for those questions that may need additional insight.

To guide the group effectively, it helps to complete each session privately before you meet together. Then as you lead the group, you can better facilitate the discussion by clarifying the questions when needed, offering suggestions if the conversation lags, drawing out members who aren't contributing much, redirecting the focus from participants who tend to dominate, and asking women for explanation when they contribute simple "yes" or "no" answers. Also, during the prayer time be sensitive to women who need encouragement or ideas for praying as a group.

For all of the sessions use a whiteboard, chalkboard, or easel pad for making lists and comments the entire group can observe. Also provide markers for writing.

SESSION ONE: *One of a Kind*

Objective: To understand what it means to be different for God.

Discussing Deborah's Story: The First and Only

1. Because of their oppression, the Israelites needed someone who could lead them in battle and conquer the enemy. They also needed a judge who was fair and trustworthy in the midst of chaos — and someone who pointed them back to God because the people "did evil in the eyes of the LORD" (verse 1).
2. Deborah was a judge, leader, poet, prophetess, wife, and possibly a mother. She was a mediator, adviser, counselor, spiritual mentor, prophetic voice, comforter, lover, and homemaker.

3. Some suggestions might be that Deborah needed wisdom, courage, stamina, diplomacy, integrity, maturity, objectivity, respectability, steadfastness, persistence, sensitivity to God, good communication skills, knowledge of the law, and a sense of humor.
4. The people weren't following the Lord, so they might have ignored his directives. They were traumatized by the enemy and squabbling with each other. Fear underscored their actions and attitudes. There may have been men who didn't like being led by a woman. Also, the Israelites were divided into tribes, which produced a complicated leadership task.
5. Suggested answers might be that Deborah lived with integrity before she became a judge, so had a long history of "right living" that could be respected; she judged accurately and fairly; she held firm to faith in God and his teachings, even when others had fallen away; God placed favor upon her; she was wise and compassionate.

Sharing Your Story: Taking the Dare

2. The two concepts can be easily mixed up. To be different for God is to follow his values and leading, to possibly be unpopular for the sake of his kingdom. The heart is humble, pliable, and focused on God. Rebellion holds the possibility of being "different for different's sake" in a way that forsakes or bends God's values to fit human desires. The heart is proud, tough, and self-focused.

SESSION TWO: *Plain and Simple*

Objective: To resolve to speak God's words as he directs us.

Discussing Deborah's Story: A Confident Command

1. Being God's spokesperson would bring favor from God and closeness to him. It would command respect from those who revere the Lord. The role allows someone to experience his miraculous ways and see people's lives changed. The pitfalls might be disdain from those who disregard the Lord; the temptation to become proud; the fear of making mistakes.

Also, because God gives prophetic and unusual words, people may think the spokesperson is crazy.
2. Deborah's words were from the Lord. She'd probably also built up a confidence in her role, and/or the impending danger compelled her to speak boldly.
3. Barak knew that the Lord was with Deborah, and he needed God's blessing and direction. He was an experienced military leader, but perhaps he also feared the enemy or wondered about his ability to lead a rebellious people. Deborah's presence would bring God's presence, and would also inspire and assure the troops.
4. Perhaps Deborah was underscoring Barak's shortage of faith in the Lord, his people, or even himself. She also was rebuking him for his lack of obedience, which God wanted to be immediate. Her words explained that if we're not willing to be used by God in his way, he can use someone else. Even an unlikely person. In this case, God chose to use a woman in a male-dominated culture.
6. At any cost, Barak still needed the Lord's presence with him.

Sharing Your Story: Good Riddance to Reservations
4. Some guidelines might be to check our opinion against Scripture; pray repeatedly before speaking up; determine whether or not we're feeling angry and punishing; think about what our relationship has been like with this person — easy or difficult.

SESSION THREE: *The Need to Lead*

Objective: To be willing to step out for God, even when others won't.

Discussing Deborah's Story: Taking on the Troops
1. Deborah cared about her people and endured hardship with them. She wanted God's will accomplished, no matter what that required. She served as an inspiration to the nation, especially the military troops.
2. Though Barak led ten thousand men, they were on foot while Sisera's troops arrived with nine hundred iron chariots. This gave the enemy an advantage over Israel, being able to move faster and with more force.

3. Barak is still following the Lord's leading through Deborah.
4. Though Sisera's troops looked menacing, the Lord was still with Barak. God had promised the battle to Barak, and Deborah's reminder was a confidence builder. God, not Barak, was in charge of the battle, and that meant certain victory.
5. Deborah had earned the people's respect as their leader; they recognized her as God's instrument. Perhaps because of the acute danger, it didn't matter whether the leader was a man or woman.
6. God uses people to accomplish his will on earth. He may also have been building their confidence as a nation and in him as their defender.
7. In the past when Israel didn't completely obliterate the enemy, the enemy and their pagan practices spiritually contaminated God's people.

SESSION FOUR: *The Big Chance*

Objective: To discern God's timing for when we're to act.

Discussing Deborah's Story: A Strike for Israel

1. Jael was brave, quick, smart, loyal, strong, cunning, determined, assertive, resourceful.
2. *(first question)* Jael was willing and available. She was also an example of how God fulfills his purpose through unexpected and unusual means.
3. God could have used someone else to kill Sisera. Or if Sisera lived, he could have gathered more troops and, later on, attacked the Israelites again.
5. The author wanted to emphasize who really led, controlled, and won the battle. The Israelites and other nations needed to know that God reigned and worked on their behalf. Perhaps the Lord even subdued Jabin in astounding ways that didn't involve the Israelite troops. But primarily, the Lord wanted Israel to recognize, follow, and worship him as their source of strength.

Sharing Your Story: Matters of Movement

3. Suggestions may be that God tells us in several different ways; the circumstances pull together in a distinctive way; our trusted advisers agree; we feel God's nudge from within, etc.

SESSION FIVE: *A Humble Success*

Objective: To give God praise for his fundamental part in our successes.

Discussing Deborah's Story: A Song to Remember

1. A stubborn people "willingly offering themselves" is something to praise God about. They are following him and expressing courage. It's a change of heart on two counts.
2. Deborah mentions God's past provision to remind them of his goodness throughout their history, and to encourage them to trust him in the future. The Lord has been faithful, even when the people rebelled.
3. *(second question)* On the surface the Canaanites had created the problem. But actually, the Israelites had brought the distress on themselves by not following the Lord.
4. It may have sounded like Deborah was boasting. Or she may have been simply recalling the facts.
6. God wanted the people to understand and recognize him as the powerful source of their strength; to keep themselves in perspective to him; to give him the credit due him.

SESSION SIX: *Good Memories*

Objective: To encourage others with how God has worked in our lives.

Discussing Deborah's Story: A Battle in Review

1. The tribes fractured the nation's unity, especially when they didn't all participate in the battle. The lack of participation could have caused resentment from those who did fight.
2. Deborah probably wanted to give honor to those who chose to fight. But one wonders if their mention caused resentment by those who didn't participate.
4. The reference to Sisera's mother reveals the feminine perspective of the author. It also emphasizes the reality and extent of the victory. It reached into the personal lives of the Canaanites.
6. God is faithful to his people when they are willing to trust and follow him. He pursues and destroys our enemies. He is our source and strength. He is worthy of our praise.

About the Authors

Judith Couchman is the owner of Judith & Company, a business devoted to writing, speaking, and editing. She is the author/compiler of forty books and speaks to women's and professional groups around the country. Judith was the founding editor-in-chief of *Clarity* magazine, and has won awards for her work in book publishing, corporate communications, journalism, and secondary education. She lives in Colorado.

RuthAnn Ridley is a freelance writer who has led Bible studies for over thirty years. She has a degree in piano performance and serves with her husband on the associate staff of The Navigators. She is the author of *God's Love* and *Knowing God Through the Psalms*, and has recently published a novel on the life of Johann Sebastian Bach. She lives in Colorado.

WOMEN OF FAITH℠

Women of Faith partners with various Christian organizations,
including Zondervan, Campus Crusade for Christ International,
Crossings Book Club, Integrity Music, International Bible Society,
Partnerships, Inc., and World Vision
to provide spiritual resources for women.

For more information about Women of Faith
or to register for one of our nationwide conferences,
call 1-800-49-FAITH.
www.women-of-faith.com

We want to hear from you. Please send your comments about this book to us in care of the address below. Thank you.

ZONDERVAN™

GRAND RAPIDS, MICHIGAN 49530
www.zondervan.com